seas and oceans WHY?

WHY DOES THE CLOWNFISH LIVE INSIDE THE TENTACLES OF SEA ANEMONES?

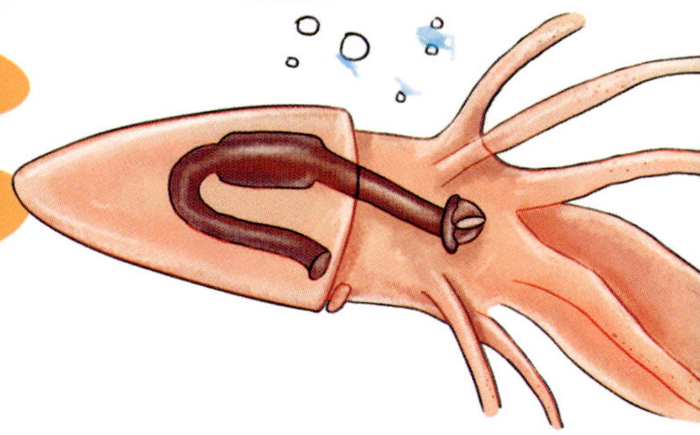

Om KIDZ
An imprint of Om Books International

WHY?

CONTENTS

1 Why is the ocean blue?

The ocean appears to be blue because it reflects blue light. Sunlight is made of different wavelengths of light. Water molecules mainly absorb longer wavelengths of light, such as those in the red, orange, yellow and green wavelengths. Shorter wavelengths, like the blue wavelengths, tend to get reflected back to our eyes. This is why we usually see ocean water as blue.

Find out!

Find out fresh water and salt water bodies closest to the place you live in.

Pocket fact

We give more oxygen!
About 70 per cent of the oxygen we breathe is produced by the oceans.

2 Why is the sea salty?

Seas and oceans are salty because they contain dissolved minerals. These minerals are called 'salts'. The ocean floor contains huge amounts of minerals. The movement of the water and waves erodes the ocean floor and minerals are dissolved into the water. Seas and oceans also get salt from the runoff water that pours into them from streams, rivers and lakes.

Find out!

How many islands does the Pacific Ocean contain?

3 Why doesn't the ocean freeze?

Because it has salt! Water freezes at zero degrees Celsius. But do you know if you add salt to it, it freezes at a much lower temperature. Oceans have a large amount of salt dissolved in it, which makes it difficult to freeze. This is because the presence of salt makes it harder for water molecules to bond to the ice structure. Another factor that affects the freezing of ocean is its movement. Unlike lakes and ponds, ocean waves move around constantly. This helps the ocean water retain its heat and prevents it from freezing.

4 Why is it warmer by the sea in winters?

Pocket fact

The temperature of air in the Arctic Ocean starts to fall during the winter months. Then a deep layer of seawater begins to develop minuscule ice crystals. This slushy water is called 'frazil ice'.

Because it takes longer for water to get heated up or to get cooled. During summer, the land near the sea gets heated up quickly but the sea water remains cool. The warm air above the land being lighter, rises up. Cool breeze blows from the sea and replaces it. This makes the land cooler in summer.The reverse happens in winter. The land cools quickly but the sea water remains warm and thus, the land gets warm breeze from the sea.

5 Why don't oceans dry up?

There are three main reasons for it – the size of the ocean, the rate of evaporation and water received from other sources. Oceans hold around 97 per cent of Earth's water. The water from oceans evaporates constantly but at a very slow rate. At the same time, oceans receive water through rivers, underground channels and rainfall. The water lost by the oceans is almost the same as water received, thus preventing the oceans from drying up.

Find out!

When is the World Ocean Day celebrated?

6 Why are lagoons formed?

Pocket fact

Lagoon is derived from the Italian word laguna, which refers to the waters around Venice.

A lagoon is a shallow body of water protected from a larger body of water (usually the ocean) by sandbars, barrier islands, or coral reefs. Lagoons are formed when sand and silt gets collected between the water on a beach or any other river body. It divides the waterbody into two or more. Such water bodies are called lagoons. Lagoons are also called estuaries, sounds, bays, or even lakes.

Find out!

Which is the longest beach on Earth?

7 Why are beaches sandy?

Sand on beaches around the world comes from the weathering of rocks near the sea. In addition to that, flowing rivers also continuously erode the rocks and other materials on land, which breaks down rocks into tiny, sand-sized particles. Rivers carry these particles along with them while flowing. When rivers flow into the sea or ocean, sand particles being heavier are deposited on the shore, thus forming sandy beaches. But this process takes hundreds of thousands of years!

Pocket fact

Wild Beach!
A beach that remains undisturbed by modern human influences such as nearby houses, resorts, shops, camps or hotels is called a wild beach.

8 Why are beach sands of different colours?

The colour of sand may vary from one beach to another. It may be pink, white or green. The colour of sand depends on the rocks and materials, which eroded to form it. White sand on tropical beaches comes from dead corals, which are made of calcium carbonate. Hawaiian beaches are colourful because of volcanic material. The pink sand of Bermuda gets its colour from coral pieces and shells.

9 Why do we name hurricanes?

To avoid confusion! Until the early 1950s, meteorologists tracked tropical storms and hurricanes by the year and the order in which they occurred during that year. But it created confusion when two or more hurricanes occurred at the same time. Sometimes confusion and false rumours also resulted when storm advisories broadcast from radio stations were mistaken for warnings concerning an entirely different storm located hundreds of miles away. So, short and easily remembered names in written as well as spoken communication were used to name hurricanes and storms.

Find out!

What are the other names of a hurricane?

Pocket fact

The Chesapeake Bay was one of the first dead zones ever identified. It was identified in 1970s. It is on the East Coast of the United States.

10 Why are dead zones formed in the ocean?

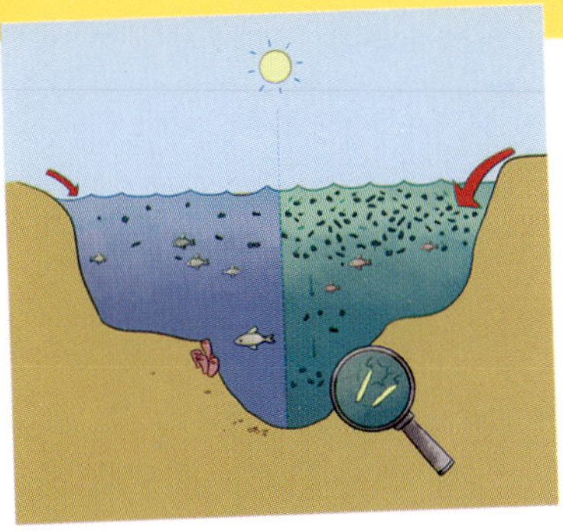

'Dead zone' is a more common term for hypoxia, which refers to a reduced level of oxygen in the water. The main cause of formation of those zones is lack of nutrients due to human activities. Excess nutrients that run off land or are piped as wastewater into rivers and coasts can cause an overgrowth of algae, which then sinks and decomposes in water. The decomposition process consumes oxygen and thus reduces the level of oxygen. This makes it difficult for marine creatures to survive, thus forming a dead zone.

Find out!

Look at the world map or globe and identify the location of Bay of Fundy.

11 Why is the water in Gulf Stream warm?

The Gulf Stream is a warm surface ocean current. It starts in the Gulf of Mexico and flows northeast across the Atlantic. The Gulf of Mexico is near the equator and tropical waters are warmer because they receive the light of the Sun at a sharper angle. The Gulf Stream influences the climate of the UK and Northwest Europe by bringing with it humid mild air.

12 Why does the Bay of Fundy have the highest tides?

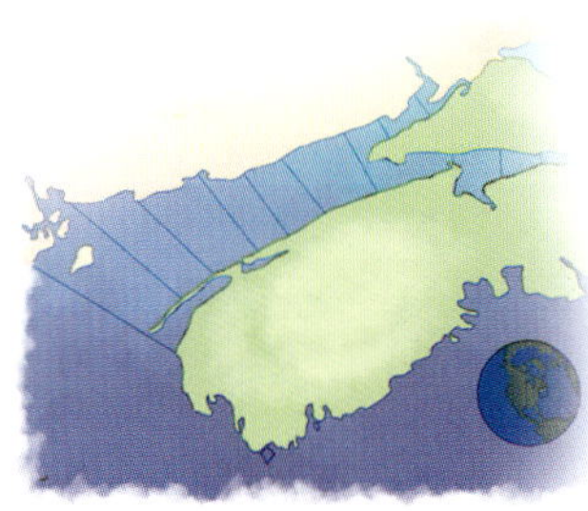

Tides are caused by the gravitational pull of the Moon and the Sun on Earth. The Bay of Fundy is a bay on the Atlantic coast of North America. It experiences the highest tides in the world because of some distinct features like a substantial amount of water, a unique shape and size that causes resonance. This natural resonance or rocking motion is called seiche. It takes about 13 hours for the water in the bay to rock from the mouth of the bay to the head of the bay and back again. As the ocean tide rises and floods into the bay every 12 hours and 25 minutes, it reinforces the rocking motion.

Pocket fact

First discovered! The Gulf Stream was first discovered in 1513 by the Spanish explorer Juan Ponce de Leon.

13 Why do seashells sound like the ocean when you hold them next to your ear?

Find out!

Which is the biggest seashell in the world?

Because they capture the sound around you! The sound that you hear from inside a seashell is the echo of the noise in the air around you. This is called ambient noise. The seashell captures the ambient noise, which then resonates inside the shell. Different frequencies of sound are echoed back to your ear depending upon the size and type of shell. This leads to different shells making different sounds.

14 Why are pearls formed inside a shell?

Pocket fact

La Peregrina is one of the most famous pearls in the world. It is a 500-year-old pearl shaped like a pear and the size of a large pigeon's egg.

Pearls come from a living sea creature: the oyster. They are formed by a process within the oyster when it protects itself from foreign substances. As oysters grow, they produce a substance called nacre. Nacre is the material that forms the oyster's shell. When a foreign particle like sand or parasite enters the shell, the oyster works to protect itself by covering the particle with layers of nacre. These layers become iridescent and roundish in shape and turn into what is known as a pearl.

Find out!

Find out some ways to reduce ocean acidification.

15 Why are planktons important to aquatic ecosystems?

Planktons are microorganisms such as bacteria, algae and protozoa. They live near the surface of seas and oceans to get sufficient light for photosynthesis. They absorb sunlight and nutrients from water to produce their own food and release oxygen in the process. About 50 per cent of the world's oxygen is supposed to be produced by photosynthesis of these planktons. Planktons are also important because they form the foundation of the marine food chain. They are the primary food source for everything from microscopic organisms to whales!

16 Why does the ocean become acidic?

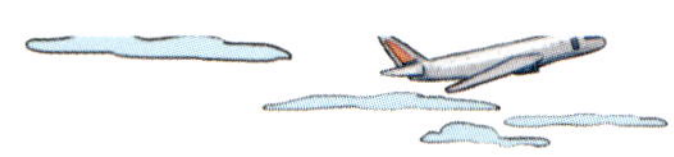

The ocean becomes acidic when the amount of carbon dioxide in the ocean increases. This is called ocean acidification. Acidification has harmful impact on animals like oysters, corals, sea urchins. It limits the growth of corals by corroding pre-existing coral skeletons and at the same time slows the growth of new ones. The acidic environment also affects fish, other marine animals and plants.

Pocket fact

Planktons are divided into two categories. The first category is small marine animals called zooplankton. The second category includes plants and is called phytoplankton.

17 Why do some deep-ocean animals glow in water?

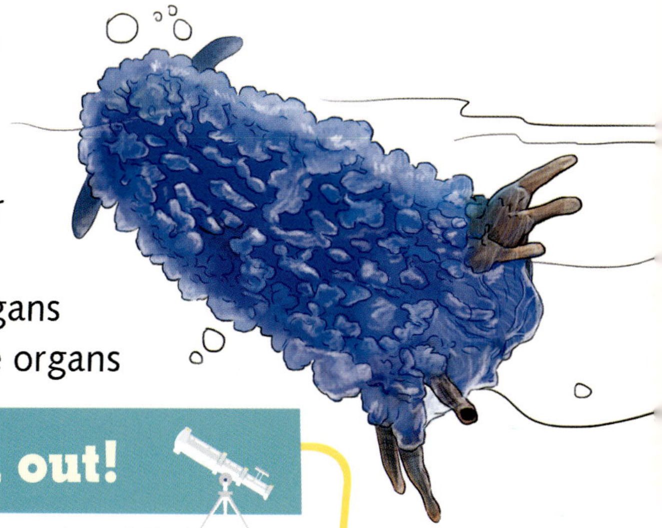

Because they produce light! Some deep-water animals known as bioluminescent organisms are capable of producing light with special organs called photophores. Light is produced in these organs by reaction of two chemicals called luciferin and luciferase in the presence of oxygen. These creatures produce light for a variety of reasons. For some, it is a warning to stay away. For others, it is a form of communication, camouflage or navigation.

Find out!

Name an insect that can glow.

Pocket fact

That's big!
The largest squid is believed to be 60 feet long with a weight of 1,000 kg.

18 Why does the food of the giant squid pass through its brain?

Because its food pipe passes through its brain! The giant squid is a marine creature that lacks teeth. It uses its arms to catch its prey and tears it with its sharp beak in the centre of the arms. It then pushes the food from the mouth into the food pipe, the esophagus that passes through a donut-shaped hole in its brain. The enzymes in the esophagus begin grinding up food into tiny bits, which are then passed to the stomach and digested completely.

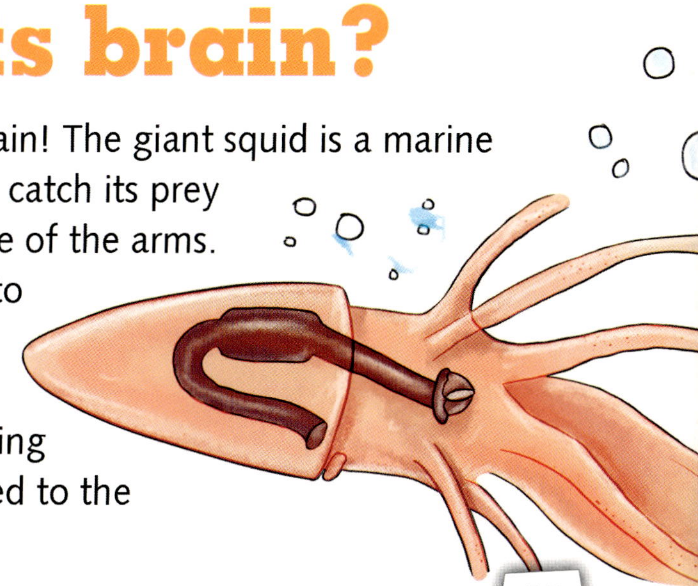

Find out!

What do dolphins feed on?

19 Why are sea sponges important?

They play an important role in the nutrient cycle in coral reef ecosystems. Sponges are small sea animals with many cells, but no mouth, muscles, heart or brain. They are important because of their role in recycling nutrients and the part they play in the coral reef life cycle. They break down complex organic material into food for other things living on the coral reefs. Some organisms cannot use food produced by corals and algae. Sponges take up this food and turn it into simpler forms. Sponges also help to lower nitrogen levels in water and keep the ecosystem clean.

20 Why do dolphins sleep with one eye open?

Dolphins shut only half of their brains while sleeping. If the left eye is closed then the right portion of the brain sleeps and vice versa. The other half of the brain works even during its sleep. It monitors activities in the surrounding environment and controls breathing. This one-eye open sleep is known as 'slow-wave sleep'. During 24 hours, each half of the brain gets four hours of slow-wave sleep.

Pocket fact

Sponges can be immensely helpful in treating many diseases like malaria, tuberculosis and cancer. Chemicals from sponges have many antibacterial properties.

21 Why does the clownfish live inside the tentacles of sea anemones?

A sea anemone looks a lot like a flower with some features like plants. But it's actually a marine animal. Sea anemones are close relatives of coral and jellyfish. Their bodies are like hollow columns with a mouth and stinging tentacles at the top. Sea anemones are found in different colours and sizes that range from half-inch to more than six feet in diameter.

Find out!

How do fish breathe?

Pocket fact

In harmony!
Some sea anemones live in harmony with green algae. The anemone provides the green algae with a safe place and exposure to light. And the algae provide the anemone with food in the form of sugar and oxygen.

22 Why do fish drink water even if water is their home?

Saltwater fish drink water but freshwater fish don't actively drink water. The environment in the sea is saltier, so the fish loses water passively. Saltwater fish take in water by osmosis through the gills and skin cells. Their gills process the water and take out the salt. To make up the loss, saltwater fish do actively 'drink' water.

23 Why is the Dead Sea so salty?

Find out!

How can we control overfishing?

The Dead Sea is actually a lake that lies between Jordan and Israel in the part of southwest Asia. With a salinity of over 31 per cent, the Dead Sea is one of the saltiest water bodies in the world. It gets only a little bit of rain each year, and very little fresh water flows into the Dead Sea. The hot climate causes the little fresh water it gets to evaporate quickly thus retaining its salt content. This is why the Dead Sea stays very salty.

24 Why is overfishing bad?

Overfishing occurs when more fish are caught than they are born. Overfishing results in the imbalance of the aquatic ecosystem. When there are less fish, the number of smaller animals at the bottom of the food chain increases. This creates an imbalance in the sea. Overfishing also causes a fish threat to coastal communities that depend on fish as their primary source of protein, especially in developing countries.

Pocket fact

The lowest point on Earth!
The surface of the Dead Sea is over 1,300 feet below sea level. This makes it the lowest point on Earth's surface.

25 Why do we need to study the ocean?

The ocean has a significant effect on Earth's climate. Oceanographers study the ocean to know more about marine life and ecosystems, ocean circulation, the seafloor, and its chemical and physical properties. Oceans control Earth's weather as they heat and cool, moisten and dry the air and control wind speed and direction. These weather patterns influence water supply, food supply and trade shipments. They also affect the growth of civilisations. A study of the ocean helps us predict its impact on our societies.

Find out!

What steps can we take to protect marine habitats?

26 Why are marine areas protected?

Never ever before, the ocean and its life were as threatened as now! This is endangering the marine ecosystem, and affecting the lives of people living in coastal areas. It is also responsible for climate change. Marine areas are protected by government organisations. This helps protect important habitats and can assist in restoring the productivity of the oceans, thus avoiding further harm to marine life.

Pocket fact

Just 100 metres!
The official maximum depth recommended for scuba divers is 100 metres below the sea. This limit is set due to the risk of oxygen toxicity that occurs at high pressures!

OTHER TITLES IN THIS SERIES